HER Funny Bu

HER unique, straight-forward & no-nonsense guide to running a business for Female Entrepreneurs - with a few real & comical stories thrown in for good measure!

Serena Fordham

Cover Design by AJ Wanegar from Farm Dog Design & Publishing

In Memory of Two Beautiful & Inspirational Women:

Sarah Ellis   &   Jo-Ann Page

First Published 2019 by Serena Fordham

This Edition Published 2019 by Serena Fordham

72 Godfrey Road, Spixworth, Norwich, NR10 3NL

ISBN: 978-1-68-747070-6

Written in Norwich, Norfolk, England.

HER Foreword

"Sorry".

Yes, I'm opening this book with an apology.

An apology for all of you who have picked this up expecting the usual boring business BS, mixed in with a lot of inspirational stuff - which doesn't make much sense, and doesn't give you any practical support on how to realistically succeed and achieve in business.

However, this is the only time I will say sorry in this book - mainly because I don't apologise for:

1. Occasional swearing and potty-mouthness.

2. Being myself and 100% real.

3. Outing the other rubbish that you are conned into believing, especially when it comes to strategies to sell your stuff and run your business.

I am a Business Management graduate from one of the top five universities in the United Kingdom, and have over ten years experience in business management, sales and mentoring. I don't know the ins-and-out of every business (as everyone is always learning), but in this book

I am giving you an insight to my experiences, and snippets of the business and sales strategies that have worked for myself, my clients and my network along the way!

With so many "experts" popping up every day, there are a lot of "naughty wrong-ens" out there who promise the world, then only deliver disappointment when they have your money! So, I want to set you straight from the start - I'm not one of these "miraculous overnight success stories" - I have worked hard, made mistakes, and overcome obstacles to become the business woman I am today.

That said, I only know my own businesses inside out, and appreciate that the only person who truly knows their own business (because it is usually and extension of who they are!) is the person who created it - so who better to know what will work for you and your business than you!

This is why I believe in encouraging and empowering Female Entrepreneurs to make the strategy decisions that will impact on their business journey (rather than forcing business strategies, advice and tactics down their throats, so in the end their businesses suffocate - and even sometimes die - because of it!)

But I'm not a negative nelly, so rather than harp on more about why I created this book (to the point that you would probably get so bored you would fall asleep!) I want to share with you a talk I delivered at the HER Business, Body and Life Conference 2019, which showcases what I believe is the most important thing all women need along their business journey - SUPPORT.

Happy reading!

Sending love and good vibes,

Serena xoxo

P.S. Look out for the <u>underlined</u> words in each of the chapters to reveal my hidden message for you within this book!

Opening Speech from the HER Conference 2019

Tell me what you think this is...

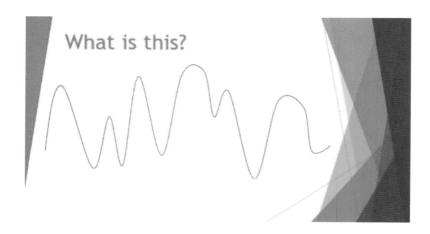

Or this...

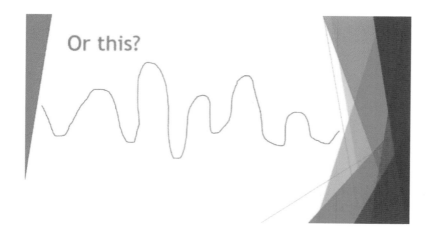

Or even this....

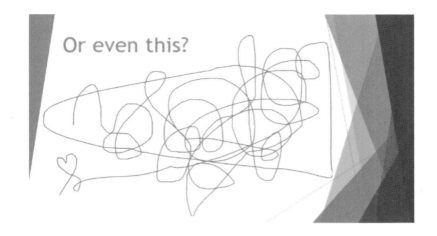

Do you know?

Well, this is the typical life of a woman - whether it be her physical, mental or emotional state - this roller-coaster line is what it looks like on a weekly, daily, or sometimes hourly basis (although as a mum of two small children, this is my emotional state within sixty seconds sometimes!)

Anyway, the peaks are when we are feeling high on life, motivated, empowered, with lots of energy, and with the belief that we can and will achieve anything in life.

During the troughs - the low energy and negative emotional times - we might feel that we are not good enough, where no matter what we do we just don't get it right, and sometimes the whole world feels like it's resting on top of our shoulders!

Plus, with lady hormones thrown into the mix, we usually send ourselves down a mini spiral of self doubt and self hate, and unfortunately some of us get even deeper down that spiral at times.

So, even though it's OK not to be OK sometimes, how do we try and stay riding the high waves and remain sitting on top of these peeks?

Let's go back to my first drawing again…

If I change each one of these ripples into trees - lots of trees in a forest that symbolises our lives...

...The roots symbolise keeping us grounded, nurtured and real. Our solid foundations.

...The trunk symbolises keeping us strong, upright and growing. Our flowing journey.

...And the branches and leaves symbolise keeping us flourishing, blossoming and free. Our passionate spirit.

You see without the roots (the troughs), we <u>don't</u> have the trunk (the journey), and thus we don't have the branches and leaves (the peaks).

So, in essence, we need the low times within our journeys to be able to appreciate and encourage the high times.

Trees also have an alternative meaning in my story.

They represent the people that are trees in my forest of life, who surround me, stand by me, are strong for me, support me, keep me grounded, and are there whether I am feeling low in one of those troughs, or high on one of those peaks.

So, my biggest piece of advice (in business and in life) that you can take away from this is to embrace and welcome everyone you meet in life, as some of these people will become trees in your forest, and also be there for you through thick and thin - and support you with whatever life throws at you!

Providing a catalyst for meeting new people and gaining support is primarily what HER Business Revolution is all about - and is also why (since launching in March 2015) it has grown to be one of the most successful and supportive women's business networks, and Female Entrepreneur training and empowerment platforms.

Because we are all superwomen

Plus, with recent substantial growth of both its online and offline activities, HER Business Revolution will continue to connect, support, educate and empower women in business into the future - with the support of awesome Franchisees to grow the network throughout the UK and beyond.

Chapter One

HER Story – Beginning With the Simple Stuff

I was on top of the friggin' world!

It all began, in 2013, just after I was made redundant from my career as a Property Manager, while on maternity leave with my first born daughter (Ella).

For some "out-of-the-blue" reason I excitedly (and maybe slightly naively!) decided to start my first business (then called "Serena Fordham's PA Services").

I had no clear direction then.

I didn't even really have any goals (and I definitely didn't have any clue!)

I just had a fantasy of what being a Business Owner was like, which was mainly based on what I'd seen in the films - you know the ones where the main character faces a few hard times, then within a year becomes a huge success and is rolling in money before you can say "NAILED IT"!

I sat at my small kitchen table one evening after Ella had finally settled to sleep for the night, and created my logo using Microsoft Paint, on a laptop that I had owned for donkeys-years. Then, I used this to pull together a simple business card on Vistaprint, feeling super "official" when I came to typing my exclusive title of "CEO" on the front of the card.

Passing these out at networking events made me <u>ever</u> so proud, and when I landed my first client - who wanted support with setting up his new Estate Agency business - I felt I had already made it big time!

Little did I know that life as a start-up was pretty simple...

Firstly, you have low expectations - so every client, every opportunity, and every win is massive!

And secondly, you only have yourself to please - no one to consult, no one to negotiate with, and no one to hold you back.

And, as my little business started to grow - snowballing from adding two to four new clients every single week - the realities of being a female Business Owner soon started to hit home.

Source: Serena Fordham - 2013 Logo and 2014 Photoshoot

Chapter Two

HER Strategy – Back to Basics

Finding Your Niche and Defining Your Ideal Client

From my lack of direction and clarity when starting my first business, I now fully understand that at the beginning of any business journey it is important to define your niche and ideal client in order to build a successful business upon.

To find these you should:

1. Really understand the problem you solve - Begin to attract your ideal client due to the problem you solve and the language you use.

   For example, for myself as a Business Strategist and Mentor, the main problem I solve is the need and desire my clients have to generate money from sales, which enables them to develop and grow their businesses.

   This problem then umbrellas various smaller problems and subjects - branding, niche, overwhelm, burn out, self-doubt, procrastination, email list building, technology, niche, launch, etc.

People will not and do not invest in you just because it is something for them to do. They invest because they know you can resolve the one problem they are currently looking for help with.

2. Identify your target audience/ideal client/niche - Warm up your audience with the language you use and the content you share.

   If you are yet to really identify these in detail, then firstly you will need to clearly define who your ideal client is (I know I said that I wouldn't apologise again in this book, but I am "kinda sorry" if I've said this before - but it is "super-duper" important, because it is the most fundamental bit of information that will determine the future success of your business!). It is absolutely vital that you are as specific as possible, and identify their pain, their wants, their dreams, their needs, their demographics, their job, what they watch/read/do for fun, etc.

   Studying this person in detail then allows you to identify the places they are hanging out right now, so you are then able to ensure that you and your business are present in these places (thus being visible to the people who are likely to be interested in what you and your business has to offer!).

3. Adapt your language when posting to different platforms, and when marketing in different places - By understanding your ideal client in detail this will enable you to really target your language to suit your niche, which will result in your audience beginning to reach out to you due to you continuing to warm them up with the variety of interesting content.

    It is important to remember that you need to communicate clearly what the problem is that you solve (rather than the solution). The problem is what your audience will be able to relate to, which makes it far easier for them to identify you as someone who is able to solve that problem for them.

    Once you have followed this advice you can then match your niche and ideal client with your personal purpose, enabling you to become clearer on the wider picture of your business, and what impact you want to make on the world by running it.

Chapter Three

HER Story – Starting From the Ground Up

My easy-breezy approach to sales was working well at that time, as referrals and networking were the main sources of my growing new client base.

I quickly learned that the more I got myself out there (cleanly speaking <u>for</u> those with a dirty mind!) the more I attracted some kick-arse business opportunities.

I'm not going to lie, this rapid success and fast growth did go straight to my head and I seriously thought I should have been nominated for "Business Women of the Year 2014", but this was my ego masking the true fact that I was totally winging it at every turn, and I had absolutely no plan, strategy, or clue what was going on in my business.

With the word "no" absent from my vocabulary, I just said "yes" to every opportunity that came my way (without questioning whether it was the right decision or not!), which meant that, with a young family and home to look after, I was on the sure fire path to hitting burn-out pretty soon!

But in the next case, in 2015, I'm glad that the word "yes" was the only one that rolled off my tongue when it came to making a business-related decision.

I was approached by a current client (whom I had been supporting with running a close-knit business women's networking meeting every month) who, due to her growing business, just didn't have the capacity to run and manage the network anymore. She invited me to take over the reigns, and I virtually snatched those leather straps straight out of her hands (like a bit of a crazy, psycho, weirdo!)

That evening I instantly began jotting and plotting all the ideas of how I was going to change, reinvent and rebrand this beautifully-boxed and packaged opportunity, and turn it into something magnificent that also suited the business personality that I had developed thus far.

As dusk turned into dawn (because I am super impatient, so spent most of that night working on it), before my very eyes "Her Business Brew", my own local Norfolk women's networking group was born.

Source: Serena Fordham - First "Her Business Brew Meeting" 2015

Chapter Four

HER Strategy – Building Solid Foundations

Defining Branding Message and Brand Basics

Did you know that over 80% of consumers are visual buyers?

This is why I rebranded the women's business network, because it is absolutely crucial to create a brand and branding message which resonates with your ideal client.

A brand also needs to offer your audience an eye-pleasing spectacle of awesomeness, which the new "Her Business Brew" teapot logo design definitely delivered, and made the network stand out from others locally too!

You can define your branding message in a short few sentences. For example:

"I am a Business Strategist <u>who</u> helps business women to succeed in, and grow, their businesses, in order to create the wealth and financial freedom they desire."

It is important that you put as much detail into this message as possible, because being crystal clear on this part of your business will ensure that you speak about what you do, and what your business does, in a much more authentic and confident way.

This message will also help you to define the other aspects of your brand, making you and your business stand out amongst other Entrepreneurs and Businesses Owners both online and offline.

Once you know your branding message you can use this to create your overall brand (that against common belief is so much more than just your logo!), which includes:

- Mission, vision and values

   Your mission, vision and values can be defined by one question - "What do you and your brand stand for?"

   Your mission is the overall aim of your business, your vision is where your business will be within a set time frame, and your values are a set of guidelines that allow your brand to meet this mission (plus aim for the vision you have set).

- Name and taglines

  Your business and product/service names can be anything as long as they are appealing to your ideal client, and appropriate for what you are offering.

  Your taglines should explain the value you are going to give to your ideal client, and give further detail about your offering.

- Logos and colours

  The key to creating a powerful logo is to keep it super simple. If you have trouble using Canva or a similar program, then just outsource this task, rather than wasting too much time on it (as it is easily done!)

  When choosing the colours for your logo (and your brand in general) select two to four colours that represent your brand and that appeal to your ideal client. Don't be afraid to think outside-of-the-box and do things differently to your competitors and others in your industry, in order to differentiate yourself and stand out too!

- Fonts

  Choose two to four fonts that you will use within your business, including for marketing purposes. Using any more than this will dilute your brand, and is likely to confuse your ideal client.

- Imagery

  It is important to remember that your brand is a feeling created over time, and is everything your clients know, believe and feel. Therefore, all of your imagery used within your business, and for marketing purposes, must contribute towards creating this feeling.

Chapter Five

HER Story – Solving Mindset Mysteries

Like having another newborn, my new network became a full-time responsibility (including the sleepless nights!).

So, in March 2015, I then had a demanding two-year-old toddler, a nearly one-year-old business, this new baby network, and a husband (that, for a man, was pretty self-sufficient, but still needed a slight bit of mothering from his wife at times!) to take care of, coordinate and nurture.

To throw another curveball into my life at the time, me and my hubby Matthew were thinking about trying for another baby.

While struggling to do up our bungalow that we had bought in an outdated and old-fashioned state in August 2014, plus also working part-time at a local Property Management Firm in order to secure a mortgage (which I bloody hated, but the people there were superb!), meant I was constantly absolutely shattered.

Exhaustion set in, and upon losing our first attempt at a new family addition, we were focusing on everything else in our lives in order to desperately bury the feelings of pain and heartache we were facing.

Even though "family-time", "spare-time" - and definitely "me-time" - were things of the past, I loved working on the bungalow and the businesses, and from seeing the incredible progression happen with all of these projects (to secure a better future for myself and my family) this made all of the hard work fully worthwhile.

As well as pushing the aching desire to become a second-time-mother to the back of my mind, I had another massive mindset killer present in my life.

I absolutely resented having to work a "proper" job.

This eighteen hours per week of pure boredom, which sucked all of the energy from my body (and the brain cells from my mind) was the one thing taking my precious time away from the things that I loved doing the most.

After only a year of working there, I was so pissed off with the place that my strong work ethic and motivated mindset to improve my efficiency and influence within my technical role went straight out of the window.

Now in favour of a more laid back and chilled out attitude of doing the absolute bare minimum, I spent most of my working day in the "day job" doing just enough to scrape by, and spending as much time as possible doodling down ideas and communicating on my phone, with the pure aim to build my own business ventures.

I'm sure many of <u>you</u> who are working in employed jobs, as well as running your businesses part-time, probably do a similar thing - but honestly this was so out of character for me, and was certainly not the "me" I wanted to be known or remembered there for.

I had always been incredibly hard working.

In school I even took an extra GCSE because I couldn't fit all my subject choices into my high school day.

I volunteered and raised funds for charities from a young age, and worked at an animal shelter from the age of eleven, of which I only left when I was fifteen to get a paid Saturday job.

While at uni (from 2006 to 2009) I juggled a full-time degree, weekend job, daytime part-time job, evening temp job, and I ran my own business with a MLM company - showing I was never afraid of hard graft and loved to be kept busy as long as I was meeting new people, contributing to a wider cause, learning new skills to better my future, and making some sort of small impact on the world.

This is exactly how I knew that this kind of "slacking-off" was very out of the ordinary for me, and totally toxic for my personal wellbeing, family relationships, overall quality of life, and most importantly to me at the time - conceiving my new baby.

Source: Serena Fordham - Awards Evening With Sara Cameron
(My "Work Mummy") in My Last Employment Before I Became
Fully Self-Employed in 2015

Chapter Six

HER Strategy – Financial Consciousness and Money Blocks

Creating the Vision of Your Future Self

We all have a vision of what we want our future to be like, and of the person we would love to develop into.

However, because of our programming, preconceptions, and belief systems we prevent ourselves from achieving this vision by telling ourselves it's hard to change.

This is definitely a "mindset-thing", and for me it became obvious that the person my "day job" was turning me into was definitely not the person I imagined myself becoming from playing the long-game.

These mind-F'ers (as I call them), plus our personal circumstances, mean that we stay stuck in the same patterns of behaviours - instead of taking the time to make ourselves consciously aware, figuring out what things are holding us back, and realising what limiting beliefs are blocking us from moving forwards - then dealing with them and changing our lives for the better.

When we take the time to discover what is going on in our internal dialogue (you know, that "little voice" in our brain that often tells us stuff that makes us feel pretty crappy!) we can then take daily actions to change what it's saying, in order to evolve into the best possible version of ourselves.

We can all reprogramme this "inner voice" by following some key steps:

1. Find your core values - First of all, discover your core values and belief systems, as it is these that are stopping you from evolving, and preventing you from becoming the best version of yourself.

2. Be visual - In order to bring your vision to life create two vision boards; one for what you want to achieve within the next year; and one for what you want your ultimate dream life to look like. It is a good idea to put time limits (or dates) against each of your vision images to give you some accountability over these.

3. Get rid of your limiting beliefs - It has been proven that our thoughts affect our feelings, which control

our actions, thus impacting on our results. Therefore, our success in business and life is basically determined by our thoughts and mindset.

In order to find out your limiting beliefs are you first need to write down what you don't want (e.g. to work such long hours in the evening), then flip this on its head to something you do want (e.g. to only work four hours each day), which will give you clearer and more positive goals to work towards.

4. Clarify your messages - When you have more clarity on what you want, you can then be super clear on the messages you are communicating to others, and also those you are sending out into the wider Universe.

   Consciously you might think you are aware of what you <u>are</u> saying to yourself (and others), but becoming more subconsciously aware means that you will then be able to engineer your thoughts to manifest the future you desire.

   Remember your thoughts create your feelings, which determine your actions, which then shows in your results; therefore if you are subconsciously thinking negative thoughts, then you will be attracting negative things without even realising it.

5. Eliminate money blocks - When it comes to negative thoughts, as business women many of these are usually related to money.

    You are likely to be carrying money blocks that you are unaware of, and even if you are conscious of the emotion you have, you might not understand the impact that this feeling is having on your ability to attract money, therefore causing you to lose out on potential earnings.

    Due to this it is important to become clear on both the emotions you are experiencing about money, as well as your beliefs around earning money.

    Traditionally, as society has generally taught Female Entrepreneurs that it is wrong to earn a healthy and strong amount of money from running a business, this has meant that women Business Owners see "money" an emotionally-loaded word.

    Hence, if you do not break this connection between negative emotion and money, then your relationship with money will suffer - causing you to face blocks of fear, anxiety, and self-sabotage, which are likely to result in you limiting your own chances of making money (mainly due to the way you communicate with your potential clients) and achieving your desired success from your business.

Chapter Seven

HER Story – Starting to Shine

As my family grew from four (including Coco the dog) to five, with our new baby boy (Alfie) born in July 2016, I had a lot on my plate.

Being in hospital for the majority of my pregnancy, and being very poorly to the point that mine and my baby's lives were both in danger, I soon became extremely exhausted and hit a wall of depression (that had resurfaced from my days of anxiety, eating disorders and self-harming in my teenage years) shortly after he had arrived safely.

To make my mental state worse, a close friend of mine, who I had worked closely with as a Director of a local not-for-profit organisation, took her own life only a few weeks after Alfie had arrived - sending me even deeper into my emotional turmoil.

To dig myself out of my slump I knew I needed a new project.

Something to take my mind off everything negative going on, and something positive to focus my energy on between changing nappies and waiting hand-and-foot on my little family.

I decided that being away from work on my short maternity break was causing my brain to dry up, and I needed something lightly work-orientated to keep my brain cells buzzing.

So, I set up "An Hour Or So", which was a project to connect businesses to raise funds for local charities - one of which was Mind, who supported those with mental health issues, as well as individuals who were considering suicide (which seemed a fitting cause at the time, due to everything that was going on with me, and with what had recently happened to my friend who was now with the angels).

I seemed to gain some comfort (and a slight thrill) from working on not-for-profit projects, and because "An Hour or So" was supporting people and charities who were doing amazing work for others, it was having an extremely positive impact on my deteriorating mental health.

While I was taking my "so-called" maternity leave (which didn't turn out to be much of a break!) I was so lucky to have been supported by some amazing women who looked after a lot of the business and work stuff, and kept the Virtual Assistant clients happy (and things ticking over pretty nicely) while I was away.

Without me really realising it at the time, this allowed for "Serena Fordham's PA Services" to expand because I then had the "women-power" behind the business to increase capacity and take on more clients.

The only niggling thing that no longer "sat right" with the developing company was its name.

So, later in 2017, after seeing a Chinese-branded washing up bottle showcasing the same name (I checked it wasn't trademarked before I used it, so don't worry!) the VA agency was rebranded and relaunched as "Glow Virtual Assistants", with the tagine "Supporting Your Business to Shine!"

A professional Graphic Designer even created the company's new logo, which was world's apart from the first logo I had cobbled together at the start of my business journey!

You see, when most women in business start out, they worry so much about reaching perfection with everything they create for their business, that they waste time procrastinating, and often take so long to launch their business (or offerings) that the whole process becomes a painful chore.

From my experience, rather than focusing on making things "perfect" and getting things "right"; I just created the business and brand; tested it; gained feedback; and refined it - all as I went along.

From this rebranding exercise it gave me the ideal opportunity to evolve my business to what it had become since I had started it - whereas if I had tried to create the business under a "perfected" brand from the beginning I might have never got round to launching it at all!

The same can be said for another project that I launched in 2018.

Admittedly I had been thinking about it for a short while (probably since the sad death of my friend Sarah, and throughout my time of declining mental health during most of 2017), but as I was then starting to feel "my true self" again, and at the same time was offered the opportunity to take over a Facebook community containing lots of women ready to embrace this idea, it seemed like as-good-of-a-time-as-any to explore the concept and turn this idea into a reality.

Hence, in January 2018 - to start the year on a high - I introduced the world (or at least the Facebook community of around 2,000 members) to the "For HER Chat Show".

Dedicated to my angel friend, this was a bi-weekly internet chat show that streamed live in the Facebook group, where myself and lots of female guests from all over the globe talked about a variety of issues affecting women.

Not only was the chat show a huge success from the beginning - attracting more and more viewers each fortnight - but it was living up to all of its promises.

From feedback gained from viewers after every show it was clearly evident that the women who tuned in 1) had developed an increased awareness of situations and issues women faced, 2) they felt encouraged to talk more openly about their own problems, 3) they saw the show as a friendly and relaxed platform to seek support from signposted organisations, and most significantly of all - 4) they embraced a more positive state of mental health.

Source: Serena Fordham - Screenshot and Logo From the First
"For HER Chat Show" in January 2018

Chapter Eight

HER Strategy – Content and Communication

Using Content and Language to Stand Out from the Crowd Online

As a Female Entrepreneur it is important that you and your business are as visible as possible (especially online) in order to show yourself as a "go-to person" in your industry; and using an effective social media strategy is one of the best ways to achieve this.

It is paramount that you ensure that you stay true to your unique self and promote yourself and your business in an original way that differentiates you from your competitors.

Social media is a busy and crowded place, therefore thinking outside of the box when it comes to your content is key to getting attention to your business.

This is why launching the "For HER Chat Show" worked so well in terms of online visibility because it showcased myself in a good light, gained regular viewers, and made a positive impact on my followers.

When you are building your brand and your business you must create leverage and credibility to help you stand out from the crowd. This can be done through highlighting your positive characteristics and achievements, which might include:

- Qualifications

- Titles

- Awards (shortlisted, finalist or wins)

- Associations

- Invitations (to events and awards, etc)

- Endorsements and testimonials

- Comments (screenshotted from social media and posted by you to show positive feedback)

You can use a variety of outputs to highlight these aspects across social media platforms; in order to interact, increase engagement, and encourage personal connection and communication with your ideal client, including:

- Live video

- Pre-recorded video

- Image posts

- Picture boards

- Question posts

- Competitions

- Polls

- Ads

- Promotional posts (although these should be used sparingly and follow a whole ton of value!)

It is also a good idea to use a mixture of the above techniques to give your audience variety, and to encourage their continued engagement and involvement (as "variety is the spice of life", thus gets rid of boredom!)

Plus, as "people buy from people" it is also recommended to turn up online on live video (or pre-recorded video if you are not yet comfortable with live streaming) so that your audience connects with you and what you do on a much more in-depth and personal level.

This has been proven as the number one powerful way to communicate with your audience because it gives them an insight into who you are, your values, and what you can offer them.

Your lives and/or videos don't have to be long, but should offer valuable tips, experiences, exclusive insight, or even be used to just say a friendly "hello!" to touch base with your audience on a regular basis.

It is best to use live video as these show you in your most authentic light, and allows your audience to better connect with you as a person. Also, they are preferred by social media algorithms, so are shown to platform users first (then video, then images, then plain text posts, and lastly any posts containing external links - so best not to use these and instead put any URL links into the comments section under your post if possible).

When preparing for a live or recorded video it is best to pre-plan a topic, then list a few bullet points underneath related to that subject.

It is advised to prepare, especially when "going live", as being in front of a camera can sometimes cause us to become "tongue-tied", to stutter or clam up, or to just forget the points that we had planned to say, which can come across as extremely unprofessional - I always follow the motto "Failing to prepare is preparing to fail!"

Telling stories is the best way to relate to your audience and encourage engagement. The type of stories you could share are:

1. Big vision stories - By sharing your big vision, dreams and aspirations this allows your audience to relate to you, and also to "think big" themselves. To make this easier, consider answering the questions "How are you going to change your industry/or even the world?", "How are you going to provide a better product/service?", or maybe "How do your products or services make people's lives better?"

2. Rapport building stories - Your stories can be personal and don't always have to be directly related to your business. They work well to gain comments

and engagement as allow your audience to take a peek behind the scenes of your professional life.

3. "Why" stories - If you are promoting a special offer, explain the story behind it, or share the journey of the process you have been on to create that product/service. This will make your audience feel inspired to claim the offer and make the purchase.

4. Origin stories - These are the stories about how your company or product/service was born, and as they are unique this means they will differentiate you from your competitors. Share stories about the experience or person who inspired you to start your company, and don't forget to talk about the purpose of your work and why you want to serve your audience.

5. Case studies/testimonials - As people trust the feedback and opinions of others, these form a huge part of the decision-making process when someone is considering buying from you. This is why sharing examples of your work, along with positive customer feedback on how you have helped or supported them with what you do, is absolutely crucial for drawing in potential new clients.

To keep life "spicy" with lots of "variety", as well as telling stories, you can post lots of other types of content to keep your audience engaged and interested, such as:

- Polls - These are amazing for research purposes, and are great if you want an insight into what your audience currently needs, their recent struggles, their thoughts on a particular product/service/activity, etc

- Quotes - Finding inspiring and positive quotes that are in-line with your products/services, and rewriting and presenting them in your own unique way under your own branding, is a useful way to encourage post likes and shares.

- Fun posts - Such as 'GIF' posts, quizzes, games, questions, jokes, etc (which are great for showing your personality too!)

Chapter Nine

HER Story – Talking the Talk

OK, so I'd started to become "me" again (well as much as I could do with two businesses, two projects, and two young children to look after!)

I began to feel much more valued in my <u>life</u> because I knew I was making a greater impact on the world. Plus, the variety in my work and home life was having a detrimental affect on my own personal wellbeing.

This was all due to the "For HER Chat Show" being a project that was extremely close to my heart at the time, as it fulfilled my higher purpose to support more women with their lives, in addition to helping them to better their businesses (which had been my only main focus up until then).

Up until that point in time I had believed the rubbish that we all get told that success is all about how much money is in the bank, and how many followers you have on social media. However, by receiving actual positive feedback from women whose lives had been changed and improved from watching the show, showed me that there is a massive difference between popularity and success.

Finally, after all the hurt in my life from the previous few years, my heart was naturally piecing itself back together as a result of the positive work I was doing for incredible women around me.

I felt truly blessed for all that I had in my life, and all that I was able to give to others.

As "giving" seems to be naturally part of my DNA, and I wholeheartedly believe that acts of kindness are a way to feel more wholesome within business (and in life in general) - what happened next in my journey hit me "like a ton of bricks".

Since 2014 (a year after starting out in business) I had met and become extremely close friends with a woman who I highly respected for her similar business interests to mine, as well as her motivation and drive to support women.

Due to this, as well as becoming close friends, we worked on a lot of projects together, and as "Her Business Brew" was beginning to expand, I welcomed her to become part of the team to support the operational running of what was now turning into a fully-fledged business entity.

This person did incredible things for the business, and supported me in taking it to the next step of its life-cycle.

However, just over a year after she had taken on the role she decided that she wanted to rebrand her own business (which bear in mind had similar goals to "Her Business Brew") using the word "Her" at the start of the new business name.

I wasn't 100% comfortable with this, especially as she had been working so closely with "Her Business Brew", and I knew that people would automatically assume that this woman's business was part of my "HER" brand, but (in order not to "rock the boat" when it came to our friendship) I went against my unsettling feelings and said it was "fine".

It was only when this individual wanted to use the same colour purple in her new branding as I was using for the "For HER Chat Show" that I had to "put my foot down".

This project was so heartfelt, especially as it was dedicated to my friend who was no longer with us, that I instantly replied to the message with a firm "no".

I explained my reasons - and then "all hell broke loose".

I was accused of being the reason why this person's business had been failing.

I was told that I had taken her away from working on her own business for my own gain (even though I originally offered her the work to support her with her income, not because I actually needed a freelance staff member!)

Then, regardless of communicating my ill-feelings about this difficult situation, she still continued to rebrand her business using the new name, and use contacts she had made while working with "Her Business Brew" to promote it.

All I can say is that I was shocked.

We had been friends for years, and overnight (because I had finally stood up to her and said "no") our friendship was over, she had stepped away from "Her Business Brew", and had also left me in the lurch with less than two weeks until the first HER Conference 2018 was due to take place.

"As quick as a flash" I felt deserted and lost.

I ended up having to involve a Solicitor, and after sending one letter to her, she reverted back to her old business name and previous branding, which showed me that my reservations about it all were validated.

The conference came and went (and was an utterly incredible event, might I add!), and a few weeks later this person turned up on my doorstep without warning.

Very confused, I opened my front door, not knowing what was going to happen next.

We cried, we chatted, and we laughed - and even though we had both been through this difficult situation of "business versus friendship" we "agreed to disagree" and parted mutually with dignity and peace.

So, now that horrendous time of "limbo and unsettle" was over, I could then start to regroup my thoughts and refocus my attention back to the "For HER Chat Show", which had then been running for about eight months.

Even though the show had helped so many women, something in my gut was telling me that something wasn't quite right with it.

I concluded that this mainly came down to the fact that it sucked a lot of my time and energy, for no financial or personal gain.

Now, I'm not a selfish person "by any stretch of the imagination", but when a project is taking so much from you, this naturally makes you quite resentful towards it after a while!

Also, as the months went on it became clear that the chat show was organically gravitating towards presenting issues that affect women in business, rather than just women in general.

So, with renaming and rebranding still fully on my mind, upon hiring and investing in a Business Coach to assist me in looking at all the bitty-businesses-and-projects I had on the go (that meant I never had a spare second in the day), it became obvious that my women's networking business (then called "Her Business Brew") should be merged with the "For HER" project (which then included a membership offering called the "For HER

Revolution") to become the almighty business that is now "HER Business Revolution".

Unfortunately, my relationship with the Business Coach didn't work out, but upon merging these entities into one solid offering it fulfilled my heart's passion and life's purpose, while mixing my love for supporting women's mental health, mindset and wellbeing, with my experience and expertise of sharing business advice and knowledge to help women grow their businesses.

Now, even though this epiphany moment and rebrand seemed to align everything I had been working on, marketing and sales were still a struggle (they had always been a constant "bug bear" for me!)

I gained some amazing knowledge and skills from completing my degree, and started my career in a very sales-competitive industry, so I have never been a shy girl when it comes to promoting what I have to offer (no filth intended!) But, with the rise of social media and online selling, this has sometimes presented challenges with marketing and selling, especially when I'm always trying to look for that unique and innovative way to get my services and offerings in front of my idea client.

To be honest, "social media sucks big hairy balls".

Yes, I really just said that!

If I had a pound for every time I heard a client answer the question "How do you market your business?" with "SOCIAL MEDIA" I would be a blinkin' millionaire by now for sure!

I just find the whole thing so frustrating, because social media is a great tool for business, however it is super busy, so unless used as part of a broader marketing and sales strategy, it is pretty useless!

The internet is such a crowded place (especially when it comes to social media) that nine-times-out-of-ten your ideal client won't see your content unless you are paying the social media platforms big-bucks (but even then, a few boosted posts or ads will not make a massive impact on your sales figures, unless there is a tried and tested plan in place).

Luckily, I realised this before it was too late (and before I had spent too much of my precious money), and created a marketing plan and sales strategy that "busts-a-big-arse move" when it comes to converting my ideal client into a valued paying customer.

But some aren't so lucky and plummet themselves into huge financial difficulty by paying for the "next best marketing fad" that only works for a short time, or never works at all.

So, if this sounds familiar to you then just avoid the next "proven-to-get-rich-quick-with-your-business" BS scam, and opt for a well-thought-out strategy to sell effectively instead!

Source: Serena Fordham - New Branding Created for "HER
Business Revolution" in Autumn 2018

Chapter Ten

HER Strategy – Growing Your Audience to Sell

Your Marketing Options and Sales Strategy

The main reason why using a marketing plan and sales strategy is so important to me?

With more and more people heading online to find the products and services they need, if you want to be successful in achieving sales, online marketing is a "must-have".

76% of UK adults use the internet to find information about products and services.

However (contradicting myself slightly), that being said, 24% of UK adults don't head online to find this info, showing that there is still a big opportunity to grow your audience and find your clients offline too (e.g. using print media, broadcasting media, events, etc).

Due to this it is recommended that a varied marketing plan is used, with a mixture of strategies that suit you (and your business) applied.

Here are some things you can do to grow your audience and customer base:

1. Create a freebie/"opt-in" with value, such as a PDF, eBook, factsheet, webinar, masterclass, etc, in order to subscribe people to your email mailing list (or Messenger Bot list). Then, create a link for your freebie/"opt-in" and share this in other groups and places online, where your ideal client hang out. Promote this on promotional threads in groups, and use story/inspirational/testimonial posts of promote (rather than just spamming the link and running!).

2. You can then use your email (and/or Messenger Bot) to communicate with your audience, where you can share more about what you do, encourage the start of conversations, send special promotions, and offer invitations to buy from you (meaning you won't always need to rely on the ever-changing world of social media to reach out to your potential customers!)

When emailing your audience it is key to remember:

- The subject line encourages opens.

- Beginning with a question engages your reader and holds them accountable to consuming the value you created for them with your freebie.

- Use one to two sentences per line so it's easily readable.

- Include your brand colours, images and marketing message that speaks directly to your ideal client.

- Add in a story anywhere you can to make it relatable and personable.

- Explain the value of working with you or your business/buying your products.

- Create excitement using language and tone.

- Create scarcity by limiting your offerings.

- Position yourself with your signature and titles.

- Repeat your call to action on several occasions if you can.

3. Consistency is key so make sure you show up regularly, remain visible at all times, be creative, have fun, challenge the norms, add value, and show your energy and passion - which should all ensure that you attract the right people to you and your business.

4. There are various ways you can grow your audience by paying - using social media ads, lead generation companies, Google Ads, Sponsorship, affiliate schemes, paid cross-promotion, and other online advertising (websites, media, etc). Whatever methods you use, you should ensure that you target the places that your ideal client sees and interacts with, and your paid promotion should always have the same call to action (e.g. visit my Facebook group, visit my website, sign up to my mailing list, etc).

5. Having a professional-looking and stunning website is key, and it is also important that it's functional and easy to navigate - with clear call to actions on where you want your ideal client to go next. The content should flow easily (in a conversational way) and naturally contain your keywords, meaning that - not only will Google and other search engines recognise

these, and show your site to people searching for them more and more (moving you organically up the rankings on search engines) - but also will mean that your reader will spend a longer length of time on each page digesting the information (thus preventing a quick bounce rate, and informing search engines that your content is worthy of reading, so they will then show your website to even more people who search for what you offer). This is what is called Search Engine Optimisation (SEO).

6. As with your website, your blogs (and guest blogs) should also contain keywords that your ideal client is searching for online. A blog is a nice way to share your knowledge, experience, and expertise, which will also help you stand out as a "key person" in your field.

7. As with guest blogging, listing your business on relevant online directories not only gives you another platform to promote on, but including your website also tells search engines that your site is a reputable source of information, so will organically move it up the rankings, thus meaning more eyes will see your website and offerings.

Launching and selling a product or service can be very tiring and exhausting, therefore it is important that you make the most of all the hard work you put in by always:

1. Capturing contact information of as many people as possible in order to follow up potential leads.
2. Recycle and automate content as much as possible.

An example of successful content recycling is as follows:

1. Write a blog about all the benefits of your offering, with a call to action to sign up to your freebie.

2. Send the blog to your email list with information on how to sign up to your freebie.

3. Cut this down into smaller social media posts with call to action to sign up to your freebie.

4. Use aspects of the blog to do live videos about the problems you will be solving with your freebie (with a call to action to sign up).

5. Send these lives to your email and/or Messenger Bot lists (again with a call to action to sign up to your freebie).

Follow up is by far the most important aspect when it comes to selling, which means that whenever and wherever you promote your offering, you should be following this up everyone who interacts, engages or reaches out from your marketing efforts.

All of your online and offline marketing should encourage the start of interaction and communication between you and your ideal client, therefore this should always be at the forefront of your mind when creating any content, and selecting which marketing options to promote your business and offerings.

It is important that wherever you are marketing your business to always use call to actions to guide your ideal client through your sales funnel, and, as soon as possible, begin a direct conversation with them to start the soft selling process.

This means if someone interacts (i.e. shares, likes, comments, follows, messages, emails, calls, etc) with your business or your content on social media, through your website, etc, then you should make every attempt to reach out to them through private message, email, or call, to begin to build a relationship with them.

You should begin any direct conversation with a friendly "hello", followed by thanking them for their interaction and then asking them one or two open questions about them, their business, their needs, etc, to show interest in them and to find out what they require.

By asking questions you can establish what solutions you can offer them, and begin to incorporate these as your conversation progresses.

It is key that you are never salesy and never push your offerings in the face of your contact. Instead always use these in your conversations as solutions to your ideal client's problems.

When your feel the conversation is at the point where the recipient seems interested in what you are offering them to resolve their problem, only then should you encourage the sale by asking them questions such as:

"Do you think this is something I can help/support you with?"

"Do you feel this will solve your issue/problem with X?"

"Does this feel right to you?"

"What are your feelings towards this?"

If the answers are negative (e.g. "No", "I don't think so", "It is not what I was looking for", etc) then remember that this is not necessarily a 'no', it means that the other party has barriers to buying from you, therefore asking for feedback (e.g. "Why do you feel this way?") is a good place to begin breaking down these objections.

If the barrier is lack of money, then either offer a cheaper alternative (if you have this) or payment plan, plus outline the value your offer will give to them in solving their problem.

If the barrier is lack of time, then either offer them something less time consuming (if you have it) or make the time limit broader (if possible).

If the barrier is something different (the usual ones are "personal reasons", "it's not the right time", "I can't justify it", etc) then call them out on this answer in a soft way, by asking questions like "If now is not a good time, do you think there will ever be a good time?" or "Don't you feel that this is worth the investment in yourself to relieve you of your problem with X?".

Be creative and always remember to sympathise with whatever barrier is presented, and offer counter-solutions to break down these barriers.

If from this process you still don't succeed in making the sale, just ask if you can contact them in so many weeks/months to see how they are getting on.

Remember that it usually takes a minimum of seven touch points with a potential customer for them to build trust and buy from you, therefore it is key that you keep the conversation open for a future potential sale if they are not ready to buy at that exact time.

Chapter Eleven

HER Story – Sorting the Spiritual Stuff

Now, the external factors of business, like branding, marketing, sales, etc, are all well and good, but I have found that on my journey in business so far - if I'm not in the best shape I can be, then my businesses aren't either!

For those who know me well, I'm not a "woo-woo" kinda person, however I do have "Romany-Gipsy-blood" and heritage, meaning I tend to be spiritually open to what is happening in the Universe.

I'm not saying that those who believe solely that success in business is down to spirituality are totally wrong (as it is up to them what they believe), however I do feel that success in business is a healthy mix of external factors (like business strategies, people and resources) and internal factors (like mindset and wellbeing).

For me, it was only when I started to realise that my personal wellbeing and mindset had a direct link to my business performance that I truly began to succeed in business.

I will tell you the story of how I came to this epiphany…

In late September 2018, following the second HER Retreat, where I had included many women for low-cost or free in order to help them out (meaning I was massively "out-of-pocket") - only for these people to step away from the network (and me and my businesses completely) based on the "advice" from someone I had once considered a true friend (and I had even become a Director of a local social enterprise Youth Organisation a year earlier, to support her during her own business journey).

I just couldn't understand how a woman who I had trusted, and who I had given so much of my time and support to, could then turn on me, and basically "warn" many of my close business contacts (who I also considered as extremely close friends) away from me - especially after I had also given a lot to these people too!

To make things even worse, on one of my "lower-mood" days (as I called them), while sitting alone crying in my car outside of the school gates, and thinking about all the incidents of "friends" hurting me over the past year, a man who was associated with this particular woman made some quite nasty and rude comments towards me on social media (and as he works in the industry of online marketing I'm sure he understands the implications of these sorts of comments!)

I instantly contacted this woman about this, almost hoping she would jump to my defence to prove that our friendship still meant something to her, only to receive absolutely no reply.

Moving into 2019, I still received no response from the woman, and as the year progressed I also found out that another person close to me (let's call her "X" to save confusion in a second) had recruited this "man" to provide marketing training for her business, when I had previously offered the same type of training to her and her team for free.

Plus, after a "heart-to-heart" chat with "X" touching upon what had gone on between me and these people over the past few months, this decision of hers just left me feeling deflated - confirming to me that there was no such thing as "loyalty" when it came to business or friendships.

So, after this harsh realisation from my "sh#tty year" that was 2018, which also included a lot of business rebranding and remodeling exercises (one of which happened at 3am one morning while on a spa break with my mum, who thought I was totally crazy at the time!!), and also grieving the death of a very close family-friend (who I felt so much <u>love</u> for, and who was taken too early after her two year battle with cancer) - it suddenly hit me one day ("like a door in my face"), while sobbing frantically in front of the bathroom mirror.

"It all starts with me".

As mascara tears streamed down my cheeks, behind blood-shot eyes was a woman who had put everyone and everything first before herself for way too long.

By burying feelings of loss from the babies that went to heaven before I had Alfie, to the grief of the heartbreaking deaths, to the hurt from the people that had used me for all they could get then pushed me aside, to the friends that had exited my life due to tough times - I knew I now needed to regroup my thoughts, and take back the power and control of my "then-confused-and-overcomplicated" life.

I realised that I needed to put myself first, step back and analyse things before reacting, take time for me to heal, eat and exercise well, and rest my constantly racing brain, in order to move forwards in growing my newly reformed business entities.

So, I started going to the gym, eating healthily (while still having the odd glass of wine and piece of cake though!), practicing gratitude and mindfulness, journaling, and meditating - all to strengthen my mindset, improve my personal wellbeing, and develop myself into a more self-assured and wholesome person - who as a result was then able to give more to the world.

Source: Serena Fordham - Behind All The Smiles There Are Times
of Tears, Frustration and Heartache

(I take photos of these moments to remind myself to appreciate the
good times!)

Chapter Twelve

HER Strategy – Practicing Rituals

Morning Routines, Mindfulness and Meditation

Rituals are a beautiful way to connect to your inner being throughout life, and are one of the most effective ways I have found to improve my personal mindset and wellbeing!

By experiencing your life in an elevated state most of the time, this will mean that you will experience more <u>love</u>, joy, fulfilment and success as a result.

As part of your routine every morning it is a good idea to be practicing a ritual that sets you up for the day, and gets you into your zone of positive mindset and heading towards the vision of your ideal you.

When we have a morning routine, it gives us a strong foundation to base the rest of the day upon because:

1. Meditation gives us perspective, and along with affirmations, allows us to feel positive about money.

2. Meditation and reflection allow us to open our minds to the world around us, and become open to new business and sales opportunities.

3. When we change our mindset about what wealth is and how we access it, we change the way we sell.

4. Journaling helps us to stay on track and makes us grateful for the sales and opportunities we have received.

5. Staying true to ourselves and focusing on our purpose, means we sell from the heart and not from the head.

Your morning ritual could include:

- Thank - Journal who and what are you thankful and grateful for.
- Connect - Use a meditation recording or song to relax and clear your mind. Meditation is a practice that will allow you to connect to a deeper understanding of the Universe, as well as giving you the ability to release any money blockages which are restricting you within your life and business.
- Move - To get motivated move around to a song you love, while saying three powerful statements.

- Vision - Think about the ideal you and the vision you have for your future self.
- Dance - Tune into your body and the way you feel, while getting your blood pumping ready for the day!
- Affirm - Write down the mantras that are important and powerful for you.
- Speak - Say desires out loud (or shout them from the rooftops!) The key to manifesting your desires is once you have set your intention you must trust that it is going to happen - so keep your thoughts and feelings positive, and this will then allow you to give off the right energy to attract what you desire.
- Take action – Once you have set your intention and connected to your vision, you now need to put together your plan of action, and break your goal down into manageable monthly and weekly action steps.

You can also use mindfulness practices throughout the day to calm your mind and allow you to receive any messages/thoughts, guiding you towards your next action steps, and allowing you to move forwards.

This is what is known as inspired action, and why meditation and mindfulness is recommended for Entrepreneurs and Business Owners.

Chapter Thirteen

HER Story – Turning the Tables

Throughout my life, unfortunately some people let me down "big-time" - and sometimes my actions didn't help the situations either (I admit it!).

But the biggest lesson I have learned along the way is that mixing business with pleasure can result in some harsh realities.

With the very personal nature of both Glow Virtual Assistants and HER Business Revolution, it is very easy to merge the lines between client and friend (and there are definitely a lot of grey areas too). Plus, being a female Business Owner means emotion and feelings definitely do come into play.

And, in all honesty, the main reason I have faced hard times - so low, that I have been found rocking in the corner of the kitchen floor with a bottle of red wine in one hand, and a full-sized bar of Toblerone in the other - was due to my emotional reaction towards the way other people had treated me (especially over the last few years, with so much personal stuff going on in my life too!)

You see, I'm a "people-pleaser", so I naturally care most about what others think about me, how they feel about what I do, and their opinions about what I put out in the world. But as you've read from my story so far, this "people-pleasing" mindset has proven to be my most destructive curse.

I have pretty exciting ideas when it comes to business (even if I do say so myself!), so when I create something new, or improve something for the better, it makes me feel absolutely awesome, especially when I then share this with other people.

But, I have found throughout most of my business journey, that after launching new offerings, I tend to listen to so many opinions from others, that this has caused my own self doubt to kick in.

Then, as a result I continuously changed my offerings again and again, to the point of pure confusion (as just went around-and-around in circles trying to change things so they suited everyone based on their feedback), and I worried so much about how others were feeling, that I didn't take a second to listen to how I was feeling.

As well as not being able to please everyone, I also realised that loyalty and honesty are rare qualities to find in people, and that a lot of people will look out for themselves and fulfil their own agendas - or be fake to your face in order to gain, then walk away from you once they have what they want - and this is especially true when it comes to business.

Due to this, I have learned not to trust anyone at face value, to question everything, and to trust my gut when it comes to protecting myself and the entities I have built.

But, that said, most people I have met along my journey have provided me with a lot of personal, emotional and business support - and, I can honestly say, that some of the amazing women I have networked with and collaborated with through HER Business Revolution have made me the much-stronger-and-more-successful Business Woman I am today.

Linking back to the "HER Foreword" in this book, all about trees and support, I have come to understand that I need people around me to survive and grow. However, it is so important to love and respect myself in first instance - and to analyse and evaluate situations by taking a step back at times, and giving myself space to control how I react.

This all comes from trusting my own instincts, practicing self-love and self-care, and looking after my own mind and wellbeing (which does occasionally involve one-or-two spa trips and weekends away with people I love!)

Source: Serena Fordham - Networking and Female Empowerment
Events 2019

Chapter Fourteen

HER Strategy – Networking and Connection

Networking Events and the Power of Connections

Whether you visit formal business networking or a more relaxed meeting, it is important that you are consistent and involve this activity as part of your overall marketing plan.

Networking is so effective as it allows you to connect face-to-face with your potential clients or others that can help you to attract appropriate people to your business (i.e. by way of referrals, collaborations, or other useful connections).

Therefore, it supports and strengthens the connections you make online, and also encourages more online connections to be made (so both online and offline networking work hand-in-hand!)

As meeting new people and networking have been so detrimental to my own personal and business growth, I wanted to share my tips to make the most out of offline networking for yourself and your business.

It is wise to:

1. Start by attending lots of different groups - of different sizes, locations, single/mixed gender, and corporate/self-employed. However, always make sure that all or some of the delegates are in your relevant target market. HER Business Revolution women's networking meetings are a good place to start!

2. Once you have narrowed down what sort of networking groups and activities most suit you and your business then be sure to find as many of these types of group to explore. E.g. If a single-sex networking group has gained you lots of useful contacts, and seems to be more suited to your product/service, then find similar groups in your target location/s and attend these!

3. Once you have attended groups that suit you on a regular basis you will begin to know which of these groups/meetings are the most successful for you, therefore these are the ones to carry on attending on a more regular basis.

4. Now you know what groups and events to attend, make sure you check out the delegate list of each meeting/event in advance, and highlight those you would like to build a business relationship with.

5. Try and chat to as many people as possible at each meeting/event, however make sure you focus on those you have previously highlighted.

6. Always introduce yourself with a smile, handshake, and a business card. Even if you have briefly met a person before it is a good idea to remain professional, therefore a hug is not likely to be appropriate (unless you are really familiar!)

7. Don't introduce yourself with a "robot-like" sales pitch. Try to mix it up a bit, and even include some personal details if you feel comfortable.

8. In conversation don't focus on the sale. It is more important to focus on building meaningful business relationships, making useful contacts, and seeking new opportunities.

9. Look for things in common during your conversation (both business and life experiences, and personal attributes) as this helps to build

relationships, and makes you more memorable. E.g. If the person you are speaking with has children like yourself, then this is a subject you can connect with and chat about.

10. As well as using networking to gain contacts, build relationships, and eventually make sales, also use groups to build your confidence by offering to be a speaker (to share your business story, or give an insight into your business/products/services).

11. Never talk negatively about your competitors - EVER!

12. A great thing about networking is that, as well as meeting new people, it also encourages referrals, which in turn encourages sales. By building trust with other business delegates, this means they are more likely to recommend you to others (both who attend the relevant networking group and who don't).

13. Always leave a meeting/event by saying "goodbye" to as many people as possible who you have spoken with. This, along with a beaming smile, leaves a lasting impression and makes you more memorable!

With the rise and changes to social media activities in recent years, the importance of connections to promote your business have become increasingly important.

Online connections are not the only ones that are key - actually the most powerful are those made offline, especially as the people you meet face-to-face are the ones that usually become your tribe (A.K.A. your biggest fans!), and who follow what you do on a more regular basis.

Both online and offline connection (and networking) support one another - as typically, a connection will start online, then will develop into an offline relationship - or alternatively, a connection will begin briefly face-to-face, then the two parties will continue conversations through online channels.

Then, after regular touch points between these people, (online and offline), this connection most likely develops into a long-term valuable business relationship, and even into friendship.

For a few of these connections, close friendships will develop (usually due to these having similar interests and life circumstances to you), and these are the people that will promote, advocate, support and guide you in life - plus help your business grow and prosper.

For some other of these connections, conversations will develop from that of a "client relationship", to possible Consultant, Recruit, Staff Member or Referrer of business/customers to you.

Due to this, it is always absolutely vital to keep an open mind when connecting, networking and communicating with everyone you meet (whether it be for business, or in more personal situations!)

Chapter Fifteen

HER Story – From Seed to Tree

As <u>you</u> might have gathered by now (especially as I have mentioned it more than enough!), 2018 was a particularly difficult year for me (both in business and personally).

I lost friends, I lost money, I lost time, and I lost a loved-one.

But all wasn't lost - as what I gained was a valuable lesson.

And, this is it...

Life is too short, so live in the moment and enjoy every little piece of it, as you never know what can happen from one day to the next!

So, people will come and go, business opportunities will come and go, days will come and go - but you are the constant - and, while saying "goodbye" to anything or anyone is usually very hard, this makes room to say "hello" to the new things and people you welcome into your life.

In the Spring of 2019 I found a new Business Mentor, who had achieved great success in business and previously built and managed a multi-million pound business - which has meant that I am now encouraged to "dream bigger" and focus on the "broader picture" when it comes to strategically planning and operating my business ventures.

I have also opened my eyes to separating friendship and business, realising that there needs to be clearly defined boundaries.

This was due to all of the experiences between "friends" I had been through, as well as (up until very recently), ensuring that one of my close friends kept her job as a priority over my own financial situation.

As historically I had always felt responsible for other peoples' personal situations and lives, I continuously put these first before what was best for me, my family and my businesses - which as a result caused me to get into some pretty sketchy personal financial issues.

The last few years have also been a learning curve when it has come to expanding the teams across all businesses.

Due to getting in some semi-serious debt (during quiet times) when employing staff, I now know that my businesses and leadership style are more suited to hiring Franchisees and Consultants, that are paid based on their performance and hard work (which is a good way of motivating the team to achieve more too!)

As well as more productivity, this type of model encourages self-motivation, innovative-thinking and more ownership and responsibility over each role - plus bringing on-board and collaborating with people who share your vision, passion and purpose, makes for a more committed and valued sense of community within each of the companies.

When it comes to business growth, Glow Virtual Assistants is steady, and gains a lot of work and Consultants through word of mouth and referrals; which makes me so humble to know that we have built an established brand, that is recognised positively for high quality output and customer service.

HER Business Revolution has been the most challenging business to grow, as moving out of area and into new territories (that neither recognise or understand the brand or our values) has proved a "trial-and-error" kind of experiment.

As we move into London, North UK, South UK, Midlands, Northern Ireland, Wales and Scotland (from just Norfolk and Suffolk) in such a short space of six months, it has become clear that there are so many variables and differences between the areas; which has meant lots of juggling, changing and refining along the way, while still sticking to a business model and strategic plan that can adapt to further growth internationally in the future.

To be honest, there have been times lately where I have felt like I am walking across a type-rope, carrying a million and one things, just trying not to drop even just one of them.

But, I've found that compartmentalising (wow, that's a big word!) my life into metaphorical (another pretty long one!) boxes, where I just select the one from the shelf that I am working on at the time, makes it all a lot easier to handle!

The stage of growing businesses from smaller enterprises to larger ones has proven the most challenging of times so far, mainly due to finding the right people, which unfortunately does mean moving forwards (and away) from people I have been heavily involved with in the past.

That said, moving on from the past is not a sign of weakness, it is a sign of strength and maturity.

People who were used to the "old me" have said that they are "worried about me", but I can assure these people that I am happier and more level-headed than I have ever been before - and that I'm sure their worry comes from the reality that they are not used to the person I have had to evolve into, in order to develop and grow personally and in business.

In my case, I think the people who knew me as the over-giving, over-generous woman who put everyone else before herself (and due to this gave most things away for free, only to be trampled all over, and this often thrown straight back in her face), it has been quite unsettling for them to witness my evolution, as they might not fully understand my need to change.

Many of these people were (and still are) extremely important to me, however because my businesses and work have become so much more than just income to me - they provide jobs for people, they inspire and empower others, and they allow me to fulfil my true life's purpose - I need to put myself first, and ensure I carry out these things in order to remain happy, and to embrace all the opportunities that come my way in the short time I have on this Earth.

When I say the last few years have been the hardest in business, I can also say they have been the most fun and rewarding!

The businesses have won multiple awards;

I became a best-selling Author (and have also written for numerous other books and publications);

I came runner up in an empowerment pageant (something of which I never in a million years thought I would be part of, let alone come close to winning!);

I hosted and ran various huge events (including conferences, retreats and workshops);

I took part in a few body confidence photoshoots (again, this is the type of thing I never thought I would do as grew up hating my body!); and,

I created a new Community Interest Company called "Mums Empowerment Movement" (previously "Norfolk Mums") that connects, supports and empowers UK mums.

This work, and these achievements, have also allowed me to source other forms of income - through funding, sponsorship and donations - which has meant that myself, and my team members, can do even more positive work towards our mission to support other people to achieve the best from their businesses and lives.

Source: Shellie Wall - "Goddess Photoshoot" for Body
Empowerment of Women in August 2019

Chapter Sixteen

HER Strategy – Business Growth and Expansion

People, Purpose and Leaving a Legacy

Expanding a business from a tiny acorn into a large oak tree can be pretty-damn-hard, especially when trying to do it all on your own (even though we are all extremely awesome "Business Superwomen"!)

Therefore, in order to expand at a faster and quicker rate you need a variety of things:

1. Time
2. Money
3. People

As you further expand and grow, machinery and other time/money/people-saving-resources can also be brought in (which, when more of these are used, usually means that less of 1, 2 and 3 are needed!)

"Time" and "money" are pretty self-explanatory, as to develop your business operations - and increase your output and revenue - as a Business Owner, you need to invest (both time and money) in developing business processes, sourcing more people to work in your business, and marketing your offerings to make more sales.

The recruitment of more "people" into your business, as it grows, can come in various forms - Employees, Franchisees, Consultants, or Self- Employed Freelancers.

Consultants and Self-Employed Freelancers are people that work with you on a freelance/self-employed basis, who - as well as taking on essential or excess workload - usually also source their own customers, and make their own sales, in order to progress and grow the business.

These can earn a percentage of sales, commission, or an hourly rate, but payment is usually linked with performance or output, meaning that there is no responsibility for you or the business to pay them if they are not generating revenue.

Franchisees are only an option for developed brands, and those companies with business models that have the scope to develop into new areas or territories.

These usually involve the business asking for some sort of investment from the other party in advance (in addition to a regular percentage of turnover or profit), meaning, as well as allowing for rapid business growth, there is less financial risk to the company if the particular new area/territory doesn't develop as well as planned.

As well as recruiting people as new team members, "people" also have other important qualities to support a business to grow.

Your existing customer base, and others who have been in contact with your business, can be used to market your offerings and promote your business, by way of "word-of-mouth" - in the form of recommendations, testimonials, and success case studies - and, because people buy from where makes them comfortable and feel good, this feeling is heightened if someone they know endorses their purchase; which is especially important in a world where consumers have so much choice.

Your current customer base is also useful in gaining feedback and conducting market research to grow your business, and can also more formally help you sell your products/services - by way of a structured and contractual Referral Programme or Affiliate Scheme.

So, in essence "people" are most vital for the sustainability and growth of your business as - 1) they can support, empower and uplift you in your life, 2) become recruits to develop your business operations, 3) promote and sell your offerings, 4) give you advise/education to encourage your business success, and 5) provide you with other valuable contacts and open up opportunities for you along the way!

Focusing on "people, purpose and leaving a legacy" (as this chapter is relevantly titled) - throughout my business journey I have been known as a "Feminist" and a "Modern-Day Suffragette", which, from looking back on my life, I can now understand why, and totally-embrace these labels with pride - as, not only do I believe in equality of women and men (thus elevating women to the same level within business and society as men!) - but I also "live and breathe" my purpose in taking a stand and fighting (peacefully, not violently) towards this mission.

After all, this is the exact reason why I set up my own "revolution" (HER Business Revolution) - with networking groups, training workshops, empowerment and wellbeing events - plus our Superwomen Membership Club, to connect, train, support, and empower women in business to achieve the absolute best from their businesses and lives.

As well as viewing this business as the way of me fulfilling my true purpose, I also see it as my life's legacy, that can be developed and evolved through future generations to come.

If you would like to be part of my "people-focused" supportive culture, my "revolutionary" mission to see every woman succeed (and achieve true equality to men) in business and in life - and you also found my business, marketing and sales strategies in this book of immense value - then you can find my full set of business trainings; along with expert advice, mentoring, support and promotional opportunities, plus lots more; in my club of talented and ambitious Business Superwomen at:

www.herbusinessrevolution.biz/Superwomen-Membership-Club

HER Final Thoughts

Before I say my final farewell, I want to leave you with one piece of advice from all that I have said previously in this book...

Do what makes your heart happy, embrace all the opportunities that come your way, learn from all the mistakes along the journey to make you succeed, develop and grow as a person (in life and in business) - and most of all, have fun in your work and play with those who are part of your life at that moment, and always enjoy the precious times with the people you treasure the most.

Money is good to have - not to buy things, but to make memories.

Time is truly the most valuable thing we get while we are alive - so we must use it wisely.

This is why I dedicate this book to my incredible husband Matthew for all his support (and supplying me with gin, wine and chocolate in times of desperate need throughout my journey), my children Ella and Alfie for being a fun (and sometimes testing) distraction when I have felt my whole world was falling apart, my mum who has been a strong female role model to me all of my life and has taught me that I can achieve anything I want to, my family for putting up with my constant business talk, and my close friend Natalie Chapman who has been there for me since the beginning of my business adventure, and is the one I can guarantee will give me a good honest talking to when I need it the most!

I hope you have enjoyed reading all about HER Funny Business!

Sending love, good vibes and fond goodbyes,

Serena xoxo

The End

Or is it?...

P.S. Did you find my hidden message within this book?

To give you a hint, you needed to look out for the <u>underlined</u> word in each chapter, and put these words together to reveal the secret message!

As another tiny clue, I have a tattoo on my inner-forearm that says part of the sentence!

If you pieced together the message, please post it, with a cheeky photo of you with this book, on...

...Facebook (@HERBusinessRevolution)

...Instagram (@HERBusinessRevolution)

...Or Twitter (@HERBusinessRev)

...Tagging in our handles, and using the hashtags #HERBusinessRevolution and #HERFunnyBusiness

If you would love to connect with me, and find out more about what's going on at HER Business Revolution, please join our community of supportive and passionate Female Entrepreneurs at:

www.facebook.com/groups/herbusinessrevolution

Source: Serena Fordham - The Most Recent Photo of My Crazy
and Lovely Family on The Weekend Away Where I Decided to
Write This Book - Less Than Two Weeks Before I Published it in
August 2019

Printed in Great Britain
by Amazon